NOTE TO PARENTS

Welcome to Kingfisher Readers! This program is designed to help young readers build skills, confidence, and a love of reading as they explore their favorite topics.

These tips can help you get more from the experience of reading books together. But remember, the most important thing is to make reading fun!

Tips to Warm Up Before Reading

- Ask your child to share what they already know about the topic.
- Preview the pages, pictures, sub-heads and captions, so your reader will have an idea what is coming.
- Share your questions. What are you both wondering about?

While Reading

- Stop and think at the end of each section. What was that about?
- Let the words make pictures in your minds. Share what you see.
- When you see a new word, talk it over. What does it mean?
- Do you have more questions? Wonder out loud!

After Reading

- Share the parts that were most interesting or surprising.
- Make connections to other books, similar topics, or experiences.
- Discuss what you'd like to know more about. Then find out!

With five distinct levels and a wealth of appealing topics, the Kingfisher Readers series provides children with an exciting way to learn to read and wonder about the world around them. Enjoy!

Ellie Costa, M.S. Ed.
Literacy Specialist, Bank Street School for Children, New York

KINGFISHER READERS

level 4

Weather

WITHDRAWN

Anita Ganeri

KINGFISHER

NEW YORK

KINGFISHER
LONDON & NEW YORK

Distributed in the U.S. and Canada by Macmillan,
175 Fifth Ave., New York, NY 10010

Library of Congress Cataloging-in-Publication data
has been applied for.

Series editor: Thea Feldman
Literacy consultant: Ellie Costa, Bank St. College, New York
Text for U.S. edition written by Thea Feldman

ISBN: 978-0-7534-6766-4 (HB)
ISBN: 978-0-7534-6767-1 (PB)

Kingfisher books are available for special promotions
and premiums. For details contact: Special Markets
Department, Macmillan, 175 Fifth Ave., New York, NY 10010.

For more information, please visit
www.kingfisherbooks.com

Printed in China
9 8 7 6 5 4 3 2 1
1TR/0811/WKT/UNTD/105MA

Picture credits
The Publisher would like to thank the following for permission to reproduce their material. Every care has
been taken to trace copyright holders. However, if there have been unintentional omissions or failure to trace
copyright holders, we apologize and will, if informed, endeavor to make corrections in any future edition.
Top = t; Bottom = b; Center = c; Left = l; Right = r
Cover Photolibrary/Wessex; Shutterstock/Charles Miller; Pages 4 Shutterstock/Dimitry Shironosov;
5t Photolibrary/Ernest Washington; 5b Alamy/Alaska Stock; 7 Shutterstock/Hunor Focze; 8 Photolibrary/
Bill Bachmann; 9t Science Photo Library (SPL)/Martyn F. Chillmaid; 9b Photolibrary/Mike Berceanu;
11t Photolibrary/Galen Rowell; 12 Alamy/Enigma; 13t Shutterstock/Yaroslav; 14 Shutterstock/Daniel Loretto;
15 Shutterstock/Yuri4u80; 16 Photolibrary/Corbis; 17 Photolibrary/ Galen Rowell; 18 Shutterstock/Zibedik;
19t Shutterstock/Jostein Hauge; 19b Photolibrary/ Galen Rowell; 20–21 Shutterstock/Yoann Combronde;
21t Photolibrary/Horst Sollinger; 22 SPL/David Hay Jones; 23t SPL/NASA/JPL/CALTECH; 23b SPL/Paul
Wootton; 24 Alamy/Gautier Stephane/SAGAPHOTO.COM; 25t Corbis/Uwe Anspach; 25b Photolibrary/
Image Source; 26 Alamy/James Osmond; 27t Photolibrary/Eric Nathan; 27b Photolibrary/Markus Renner;
28 Photolibrary/Robert Harding; 29t SPL/Jim Reed; 29b Photolibrary/Walter Bibikow; all other images
from the Kingfisher Artbank.

Contents

What is the weather today?

Have you looked outside today? Is the Sun shining brightly, or is the sky covered with clouds? Is it pouring rain, or is snow falling? Is the **wind** whistling around, or is there no wind at all? Your weather can be sunny, cloudy, rainy, snowy, or a few of these things at once!

When the weather is sunny,
it is fun to play outside.

When it rains, you need a raincoat, boots, and an umbrella.

The weather changes every day. And it affects what we wear and what we do. Do you need an umbrella or a sun hat today? On a sunny day, you might stay outdoors longer than on a snowy day. Weather is important for people who work outside. Their safety can be at risk in very bad weather.

Fishermen work at sea even in very windy weather.

Air and the atmosphere

Satellite

Space shuttle

Aurora lights

Shooting stars

Weather balloon

Airplane

Weather

Air is all around you. It is made up of gases you cannot see or smell. But you can feel the air when you move fast. You can feel it as wind too.

Air is also called the **atmosphere**. The atmosphere reaches several hundred miles above Earth. Weather happens in the part of the atmosphere that is closest to the ground.

There is activity all through the atmosphere.

Temperature

The **temperature** of something is how hot or cold it is. Temperature is another important part of the weather. Your day may be hot or cold in addition to being sunny, cloudy, rainy, or snowy.

The atmosphere is like a blanket that warms Earth. It catches heat from the Sun. The Sun also heats the ground. The ground heats the air or atmosphere above it. Weather on Earth would be much colder without the atmosphere.

This photograph taken from space shows the atmosphere around Earth.

When the wind blows

The wind is moving air. Sometimes it moves gently, like a breeze. Sometimes it moves with the force of a powerful storm. The Sun causes wind to happen. The Sun heats the air near the ground and the hot air rises. Cooler air flows in to take its place. That is the wind.

Sea breeze

On a sunny day at the beach, heated air over the sand rises. Cooler air from over the sea moves toward land, making a breeze.

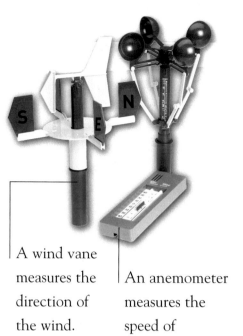

A wind vane measures the direction of the wind.

An anemometer measures the speed of the wind.

Measuring the wind

We can measure the speed of the wind in miles (or kilometers) per hour. We can also figure out if the air is coming from the north, south, east, or west.

Sometimes a huge area of warm air meets a huge area of cold air. Where the warm air and cold air meet, clouds form and rain falls.

Clouds forming above Earth, photographed from space

Clouds

A cloud is made up of millions of tiny water droplets or millions of tiny **ice crystals**.

Cirrus clouds are wispy clouds high in the sky. They can be a sign that the weather is changing.

Where do the water droplets and ice crystals come from? There is always some water in the air. It is an invisible gas called **water vapor**. It comes from the water in the oceans and in the ground. The water droplets and ice crystals form clouds when the water vapor cools down.

Strange clouds

Sometimes you see clouds with strange shapes in the sky. The clouds in this picture are called lenticular clouds. People sometimes think they are flying saucers!

Clouds come in all sorts of shapes and sizes. Some are fluffy, some are flat, and some are wispy. Some are low in the sky, and some are very high. Different sorts of clouds bring different sorts of weather.

Cumulonimbus clouds bring rain, thunder, and lightning.

Stratus clouds are flat clouds that often bring rain.

Rain and snow

When the water droplets or ice crystals in clouds grow large enough, they fall to the ground as rain or snow. Some rain starts as ice crystals. The ice crystals melt as they fall through the air. They turn into water by the time they reach the ground. When ice crystals fall without melting, we get snow!

Water vapor cools and makes clouds.

This rain is made up of big drops of water. Heavy rain like this often causes **floods**.

Water **evaporates** from seas, lakes, and rivers.

Snowflakes

Snowflakes grow inside very cold clouds. They start off as tiny ice crystals and then get larger and larger. Every snowflake has six sides.

Water is always moving between the land, the seas, and the air. This movement is called the **water cycle**. The diagram below shows how the water cycle works.

Rain falls from the clouds.

Rainwater runs into rivers and back to the sea.

Water soaks into the ground.

Lightning and thunder

A flash of lightning is a spectacular sight. Lightning comes from giant storm clouds, called cumulonimbus clouds. They are full of water droplets and ice crystals. Inside the cloud, super-strong winds toss the water and ice up and down.

Storm clouds can be over 9 miles (15 kilometers) tall!

The water and ice crash into each other. This makes electricity in the cloud. When there is too much electricity for the cloud to hold, the electricity jumps to the ground, making a giant spark. This is lightning.

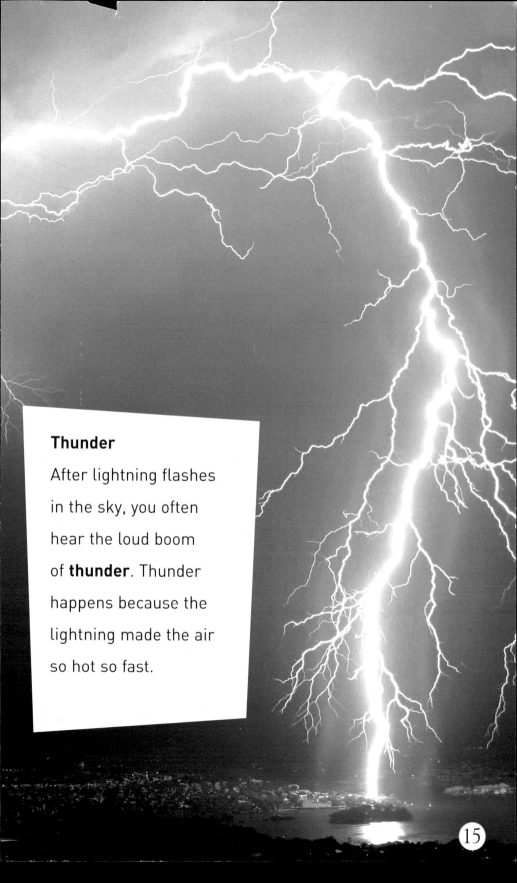

Thunder

After lightning flashes in the sky, you often hear the loud boom of **thunder**. Thunder happens because the lightning made the air so hot so fast.

15

Tornadoes and hurricanes

A spinning funnel of air comes down from a dark storm cloud. As it touches the ground, dust and much bigger objects are swept up. Cars are thrown around like toys, and houses are torn to pieces. It's a **tornado**!

Tornado Alley

The Midwest gets more tornadoes every year than the rest of the world combined! The area is called Tornado Alley.

This boat was washed ashore by
huge waves caused by a hurricane.

Inside a tornado, winds can blow at more
than 250 miles (400 kilometers) per hour.
The winds can be strong enough to lift
up trains!

Other huge storm clouds travel over the
oceans. The storms are called **hurricanes**,
cyclones, or typhoons. A hurricane brings
super-strong winds and heavy rain. A
hurricane can cause billions of dollars in
damage to places it strikes.

Colors in the sky

Sometimes, if the Sun shines while it rains, you can see a rainbow.

What makes a rainbow? Sunlight is made up of many colors mixed together. When the Sun shines through raindrops, the raindrops split the light into separate colors. The colors appear in the sky as a rainbow.

Other times, the Sun looks red when it sets. It looks red because only the red light from the Sun can be seen through the atmosphere at that time.

Lights in the sky

Beautiful patterns of light appear in the sky near Earth's **poles**. They are called aurorae (say "or-ROAR-ree"), or the northern lights and southern lights.

On some days, hot or cold layers of air form near the ground or above the water. The air bends the light from objects that are far away. This makes the objects appear in the sky! It can also make the sea look like the ground. This effect is called a **mirage**.

What looks like land in this picture is not really there. It is a mirage made by warm air above the water.

19

Some world weather records

The hottest temperature ever recorded was 136°F (58°C) in El Azizia, Libya. The coldest was –128°F (–89°C) in Antarctica. And Cherrapunji, India, has the most rain every year. More than 393 inches (10 meters) fall there!

The driest place on Earth

The Atacama Desert in Chile is the driest place on Earth. In order to be considered a desert, a place must receive less than 10 inches (25 centimeters) of rain a year. There are places in the Atacama Desert where rain has not fallen at all for hundreds of years!

Weird weather

Hail is made from lumps of ice that fall from storm clouds. Hailstones form when water droplets freeze together in very cold clouds. Most hailstones are smaller than peas, but sometimes they can be as big as coconuts!

Big hailstones like these can damage crops, buildings, and cars.

It's raining fish!

In 2010, hundreds of small fish fell from the sky onto the town of Lajamanu in Australia! Experts think a tornado sucked the fish up with water from a river.

Recording the weather

Every day, scientists all over the world record what the weather is like. They use instruments to measure temperature, the amount of rainfall, and the speed and direction of the wind. They measure the hours of sunshine and how cloudy the sky is.

This scientist is checking weather information.

This map was made using information from weather radar. The orange areas show where the winds are the strongest.

Weather balloons, **satellites**, and **radar** are all instruments that record weather information. Weather balloons carry measuring instruments into the atmosphere. Satellites take photographs of clouds from space. Radar can show where it is raining or windy.

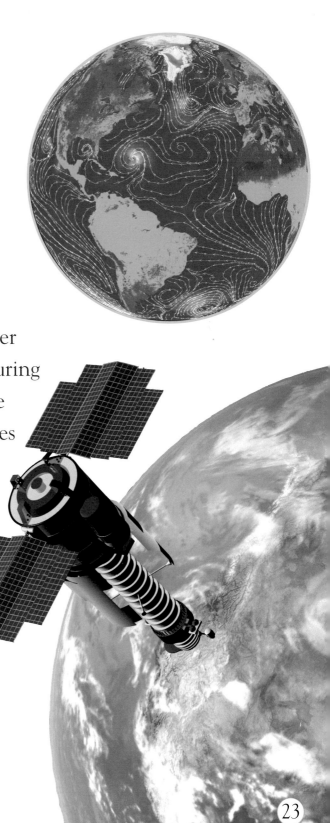

A weather satellite high above Earth, ready to take pictures

23

Weather forecasting

How do **weather forecasters** know what the weather is going to be like?

First, forecasters look at the current weather. They get information about it from weather stations, weather balloons, satellites, and radar. Then they use computers to help them figure out how the weather might change. It is very hard to forecast the weather. Sometimes even computers get it wrong.

A forecaster studies satellite photographs.

Weather computers

Weather computers use information about the current weather to work out what the weather will

be like over the next few days.

You can find out what the weather forecasters are predicting by watching television or listening to the radio. You can find out in a newspaper or by going online. Forecasters issue a severe weather warning when they predict strong winds or very heavy rain or snow is on the way.

This television forecaster talks about weather on the West Coast.

Patterns in the weather

The weather often changes from one day to the next day. But sometimes the same pattern of weather happens day after day. For example, in places near the **equator**, it always rains in the afternoon.

This is the same field in spring, summer, fall, and winter.

Most places have seasons. This means the weather is different at different times of the year.

Climate is the word used to describe the normal weather in a place. Here are four climates:

- Polar: cold all year round, with long, very cold winters.

- Temperate: four seasons, with a cool winter and a warm summer.

- Tropical: hot and wet all year round.

- Desert (pictured): dry, with less than 10 inches (25 centimeters) of rain a year.

Climate change

Many scientists think the planet is getting too warm too quickly. They think too many gases from the fuels we use have been going into the air and making it hotter. Icebergs and glaciers are beginning to melt!

Surviving in the weather

What do you do if the weather is really hot? You can wear loose, thin clothes to keep you cool. A hat and sunscreen will protect you from the Sun's harmful rays. In very hot countries, people often live in stone houses to help keep cool. They also stay indoors in the middle of the day.

Loose clothes keep the Sun's rays out but let cool air in.

This hole in the ground is a tornado shelter.

What would you do in a hurricane or tornado? When a hurricane is coming, people stay indoors and cover their windows with boards to keep them from breaking. In places where there are lots of tornadoes, people have underground tornado shelters.

Animals and plants are especially **adapted** for the climate they live in. For example, animals in cold climates have thick fur that keeps them warm. Some animals, such as grizzly bears, sleep in warm dens during the coldest months.

This cactus and prickly pear can grow in the desert even though there is very little water there.

Glossary

adapted suited to the place where a plant or animal lives

atmosphere the layer of air around Earth

climate the normal weather in a place

equator an imaginary line around the middle of Earth

evaporates when water turns to water vapor

floods when rivers break their banks and flow over dry land

hurricanes dangerous storms that bring strong winds and heavy rain

ice crystals tiny pieces of ice

mirage a trick of the eyes that happens when light is bent by layers of air near the ground or water

poles the places farthest north and south on Earth

radar an instrument that shows the location of faraway objects

satellites instruments that move around Earth in space

temperature how hot or cold something is

thunder a loud rumble made by a flash of lightning

tornado a spinning funnel of air that touches the ground

water cycle the movement of water between the atmosphere, the oceans, and the land

water vapor water when it has turned into a gas

weather balloons big balloons that carry weather instruments up into the atmosphere

weather forecasters people who predict what the weather will be like in the future

wind air that is moving

Index

If you have enjoyed reading this book, look out for
more in the Kingfisher Readers series!

KINGFISHER READERS: LEVEL 1

Baby Animals
Butterflies
Colorful Coral Reefs
Jobs People Do
Snakes Alive!
Trains

KINGFISHER READERS: LEVEL 2

What Animals Eat
Your Body

KINGFISHER READERS: LEVEL 3

Dinosaur World
Volcanoes

KINGFISHER READERS: LEVEL 4

Pirates
Weather

KINGFISHER READERS: LEVEL 5

Ancient Egyptians
Rainforests

For a full list of Kingfisher Readers books, plus
guidance for teachers and parents and activities
and fun stuff for kids, go to the Kingfisher Readers
website: www.kingfisherreaders.com